HABEAS CORPUS

PRAISE FOR *HABEAS CORPUS*

"Cindy Hochman's playful exuberance shines through each of her poems, putting the poet's personality at the center of her work. She delights in verbal nuance, and it's contagious. She aims to entertain, a rarity these days. And, her aim is true."
—Eric Greinke

"Cindy Hochman's *Habeas Corpus* is one of the most original and exquisite books of poetry I've read this year. Irreverent, yet tender, fiercely candid, she is a joyful juggler of wordplay, and her poem "Legs" in this collection is a perfect example of this poet's great talent."
—Laura Boss
Author: *Flashlight* (Guernica Editions)
Editor, *Lips*

"In *Habeas Corpus*, Cindy Hochman's witty sense of humor and joy for life shines. There's nostalgia for when she'd *fall down on her sweet knees . . . jackknifed and splayed with no spider veins*—her *precious legs in assorted beds*. At the same time, a sadness that her womb, which has *gone many places*, has never gone to the maternity ward. But, mostly, there is joy in the body, with its *fingers dialing her imaginary lover*. There is great love of life, and she takes us along with an always fascinating trip thru the body—the poems are fun, but also sadly moving—always entertaining. I love them."
—Lyn Lifshin
Author: *Malala* (Poetic Matrix Press) and
A Girl Goes Into the Woods (NYQ Books)

Habeas Corpus
Copyright © 2015 Cindy Hochman
Paperback ISBN: 978-1-941783-02-3

All rights reserved: except for the purpose of quoting brief passages for review, no part of this book may be reproduced or transmitted in any form or by any means, electronic or mechanical, including photocopying, recording, or by any information storage and retrieval system, without permission in writing from the publisher.

Cover art: Tracy McQueen
Design, Layout & Cover Design: Steven Asmussen
Author Photo: Karen Neuberg

Glass Lyre Press, LLC.
P.O. Box 2693
Glenview, IL 60026

www.GlassLyrePress.com

HABEAS CORPUS

POEMS BY
CINDY HOCHMAN

Acknowledgments

Grateful acknowledgment is made to publisher extraordinaire Ami Kaye and the staff at the lovely journal *Pirene's Fountain* for publishing the poems "Legs" and "Full Body Scan" (in slightly different form/different title) and to Glass Lyre Press for giving this chapbook a loving home.

Big "barbaric yawp" shout-out to Karen Neuberg, Bob Heman, Brenda Gannam, Erika Dagnino (*mia bella sorella*), Patricia Carragon, Evie Ivy, Ann Cefola, Amy Barone, Leslie Prosterman, and my multi-talented comrades on the New York City poetry circuit for supporting my work and refraining from throwing tomatoes at me during poetry readings, even when the puns get out of hand.

Humongous thanks to my "heavyweight poet" blurbists, Eric Greinke, Laura Boss, and Lyn Lifshin, for their kind words.

For the world, I pray for peace.

This book is dedicated to my beautiful and utterly amazing mom, Jean Keller Sostchen, whose love and devotion have always carried me through. I love you so dearly!

And in memory of my dad, William Sostchen, and brother, Rick Sostchen—I carry you both in my heart wherever I go.

Habeas Corpus, literally in Latin ***you have the body***, is a term that represents an important right granted to individuals in America. Basically, a *writ of habeas corpus* is a judicial mandate requiring that a prisoner be brought before the court to determine whether the government has the right to continue detaining them. In the throes of the American Civil War, President Abraham Lincoln took a lot of flak for suspending it.

For the sake of this chapbook, however, you only have to remember the *you have the body* part.

Contents

Womb	15
Legs	16
Tongue	17
Mouth	18
Liver	19
Fingers	20
Eyebrows	21
Heart (a sonnet)	22
Mind	23
Eyes	24
Ears	25
Ears (revised)	25
Breasts	26
Full Body Scan	27

Womb

Eve didn't know her asp from her elbow because she was too busy tendon her garden. My own weeded womb has gone many places, except the maternity ward.

I'm alone in my womb.

Legs

Back when I was ether-eyed and doe-legged, back with my Buddha breaths and a little pastel heart, back with my unruly mop of wild wheat hair and unholy mess of wild thoughts, back when my home was the porcelain throne, back when I smelled of sea-spray and foam, back when I had a quick trigger tongue, back when I was not so wound up and not so wounded, back when I'd fall down on my sweet knees and say *god bless these moon-thin legs*, jackknifed and splayed, with no spider veins—my precious legs in assorted beds.

Tongue

This tongue has said *hello* to God—and *good-bye* to Dad.

Mouth

Cluck and chatter. Boy-kisses, mouthful of roses. Later, cocks of the walk (an oral history). After that, foot in mouth (oops!). It's feeding time at the zoo, but there's nothing left in the trough. And there's no such thing as a boxed lunch. Oh, let me eat cake before I march off to the guillotine (no appetite for war). Burble, babble, and gorge. Shut like a timid clam or singing like a blue canary. Pretty mouth, pouty mouth, putty mouth, poet mouth. Me speak with forked tongue lolling in my mouth. Let me throw my sins and cusses into the Hudson River. Into the Finger Lakes. Into Montego Bay. Into the Atlantic Ocean. Mouth full of ice pops and Sheetrock and snowflakes. Vodka laced with Valium. Brickbats and boll weevils. And anything else I can cram (shove) (stuff) into this ravenous mouth. Venomous mouth. Unquenchable mouth.

Liver

I had to give up drinking because it's a sin tequila mockingbird.

Fingers

What a thrill / My thumb instead of an onion
—"Cut," by Sylvia Plath

Twiddle and Twitter and trace. Fingers are everywhere these days—it's a digital world. There are tables full of finger food and it's finger-lickin' good. Every finger wants to be a steeple or a temple or a little teapot. Everyone wants to have warm and holy fingers, thumbs up or thumbs down. Little fingers playing pick-up sticks and jacks. My clumsy fingers dropping the ball. Do you have sticky fingers, stinky fingers, or extra fingers like Hemingway's cats? According to Plath, a severed thumb is a joy forever. Did you lose your finger in the war? I lost mine at Niagara Falls. When he slipped that lethal ring around my golden finger, it turned a mad blue. If I snap my fingers, will you come? One finger on the pulse and one on the trigger. Beware the full lunula—you don't know what these crazy fingers can do. Fingers strumming my imaginary guitar, dialing my imaginary lover, counting my imaginary dough. Arthritic fingers turning the vintage page. Here's to the middle finger, the victory fingers, the ones that call *time*, and the ones that say *peace*. Get your greedy fingers out of the pie and your haughty finger out of my face. Stop picking those blistered fingers; stop biting those nails. Can't you lift a finger? Didn't your mama ever tell you it's not nice to point?

Eyebrows

After the chemo zapped my eyebrows to Kingdom Come, I took my kohl black pencil and drew an arched and defiant line in the sand.

Heart (a sonnet)

Except for the occasional heart attack, I never felt better.
—Dick Cheney

Dick Cheney got a new heart. To replace the one he was missing at birth.
Dick Cheney got a new heart. It's red like the devil's horns on his head.
Dick Cheney got a new heart. So he can triple bypass the abject poor.
Dick Cheney got a new heart. He can jog—but, for God's sake, don't let him run.
Dick Cheney got a new heart. It has no left atrium and no left ventricle.
Dick Cheney got a new heart. It has four fully loaded echo chambers.
Dick Cheney got a new heart. It ticks like a weapon of mass deconstruction.
Dick Cheney got a new heart. He invented the term *A-fib*.
Dick Cheney got a new heart. With a sticker that says *I Heart Halliburton*.
Dick Cheney got a new heart. It beats like the one in *The Wizard of Oz*.
Dick Cheney got a new heart. How about a little waterboarding, Scarecrow?
Dick Cheney got a new heart. But I don't think he'll send me a valentine this year.
Dick Cheney got a new heart. As the guilty donor sighs in his grave.
Dick Cheney got a new heart. Let him live and be well . . . and shut his heartless mouth.

Mind

What a waste it is to lose one's mind. Or not to have a mind is being very wasteful. How true that is.
—Dan Quayle

My mind is a minefield. My mind is a gold mine, a coal mine (open pit, toxic abyss). Freud would have a field day down in my diamond mind. My mind is not mine. My inner toddler, she sticks out her tongue and kicks me in the shins. I know that I'm left-brain dominant because I always vote for the Democrats. Even when they raise my taxes. My mind is a bird in the hand, two birds in my bush. No butterflies in my inkblots—just bullseyes and firing squads, the battlefield at Gettysburg, and the occasional cigar. My mind is an electric chair at the moment of jolt. My mind is the great executioner and I am its last meal. I wish my mind were peaceful as Pan's magic lyre, but it marches all day like a mariachi band. I wish my Rorschach would bring me roses. I wish I didn't have bats in my belfry. I wish my mind were a Hallelujah Chorus of calm. My mind is from Venus; yours, from Uranus. My mind is a Virgo with agoraphobia rising. I lose my mind a lot, especially the third Wednesday of every month. But then I look behind the fridge—and there it is.

Eyes

Part I.

Don't preach to me with your evangelist eyes, don't Google me with your eBay eyes, don't eye me with your iPhone eyes, don't Scrooge me with your Ebenezer eyes, don't sadden me with your elegiac eyes, don't field me with your Elysian eyes, don't corner me with your edgy eyes, don't monkey me with your evolutionary eyes, don't con me with your easy-street eyes, don't boss me with your executive eyes, don't fire me with your ember eyes, don't judge me with your ecclesiastical eyes, don't forsake me with your *Elohim* eyes, don't leave me with your emeritus eyes, don't scare me with your end-times eyes, don't end me with your epilogue eyes.

Part II.

Edit me with your eagle eyes, em dash me with your Emily eyes, dot me with your ellipsis eyes, tease me with your Earl Grey eyes, salute me with your enlisted eyes, be there or be square with your early-bird eyes, charge me with your Eveready eyes, prove it with your empirical eyes, equalize me with your egalitarian eyes, Last Supper me with your Easter eyes, lava me with your earthquake eyes, swallow me with your esophageal eyes, undress me with your Edwardian eyes, sing my body with your electric eyes, enter me with your erectile eyes, "F" me with your effin' eyes, gouge me with your Oedipal eyes, remember me with your eulogy eyes.

Ears

~~Well, they don't stick out as far as Barack Obama's and they're not as depressed as Van Gogh's. They weren't found in a grassy knoll à la *Blue Velvet*. I was struck Beethoven-deaf from the first row of The Who and Led Zep. Oh, if I only had a hammer and an anvil. Can you hear me now? CAN YOU HEAR ME NOW? Yes, I can, but I think I've heard enough already.~~

Ears
(revised)

I wrote a poem about EARS, but like Van Gogh's, it ended up on the cutting room floor.

Breasts

Breasts revisited. One lump, over the hump. No longer the carcinogenic bride.

Full Body Scan

None of my wounds are superficial. Burned fingers, bullet holes. Gash, gauze, guns. Spilled guts, split lip, slipped disc, slashed tires, surgical mask, stomach pump, siren's song, stigmata. Hair of the dog, *habeas corpus*, head through glass (sweep away blood). Chronic choke. False teeth in Dixie cup, rotten teeth in mouth, face in soup. Roses in room. (*Insurance, please!*) Electric shock/electroshock. Epinephrine. Next of kin. Cherry bomb. Air raid. Code Blue, Code Red. None of my wounds are superficial (am I dying for my art?) Tell me: Which is the nurse's button? Which is the nuclear button? Which is the panic button?

I think I shall make an exquisite corpse!

GLASS LYRE PRESS, LLC
"exceptional works to replenish the spirit"

Poetry Collections
Poetry Chapbooks
Select Short & Flash Fiction
Anthologies

Glass Lyre Press is an independent literary publisher interested in technically accomplished, stylistically distinct, and original work. Glass Lyre seeks diverse writers that possess a dynamic aesthetic, and an ability to emotionally and intellectually engage a wide audience of readers.

Glass Lyre's vision is to connect the world through language and art. We hope to expand the scope of poetry and short fiction for the general reader through exceptionally well-written books, which evoke emotion, provide insight, and resonate with the human spirit.

www.GlassLyrePress.com